DISCARD

EXPLORING THE STATES

Maine

THE PINE TREE STATE

by Patrick Perish

BELLWETHER MEDIA • MINNEAPOLIS, MN

Note to Librarians, Teachers, and Parents:

Blastoff! Readers are carefully developed by literacy experts and combine standards-based content with developmentally appropriate text.

Level 1 provides the most support through repetition of high-frequency words, light text, predictable sentence patterns, and strong visual support.

Level 2 offers early readers a bit more challenge through varied simple sentences, increased text load, and less repetition of high-frequency words.

Level 3 advances early-fluent readers toward fluency through increased text and concept load, less reliance on visuals, longer sentences, and more literary language.

Level 4 builds reading stamina by providing more text per page, increased use of punctuation, greater variation in sentence patterns, and increasingly challenging vocabulary.

Level 5 encourages children to move from "learning to read" to "reading to learn" by providing even more text, varied writing styles, and less familiar topics.

Whichever book is right for your reader, Blastoff! Readers are the perfect books to build confidence and encourage a love of reading that will last a lifetime!

This edition first published in 2014 by Bellwether Media, Inc.

No part of this publication may be reproduced in whole or in part without written permission of the publisher. For information regarding permission, write to Bellwether Media, Inc., Attention: Permissions Department, 5357 Penn Avenue South, Minneapolis, MN 55419.

Perish, Patrick.
 Maine / by Patrick Perish. – (Blastoff! readers. Exploring the states)
  pages cm. – (Blastoff! readers. Exploring the states)
 Includes bibliographical references and index.
 Summary: "Developed by literacy experts for students in grades three through seven, this book introduces young readers to the geography and culture of Maine"–Provided by publisher.
 ISBN 978-1-62617-018-6 (hardcover : alk. paper)
 1. Maine–Juvenile literature. I. Title.
 F19.3.P47 2014
 974.1–dc23
                                                                                    2013008236

Printed in the United States of America, North Mankato, MN.

Table of Contents

Where Is Maine?

Maine is located in the northeast corner of the United States. It is one of the **New England** states. Northwest of Maine lies the Canadian **province** of Quebec. On the northeastern side is the province of New Brunswick. New Hampshire is Maine's neighbor to the west.

Maine has nearly 3,500 miles (5,633 kilometers) of coastline along the Atlantic Ocean. The state capital is Augusta. It sits on the Kennebec River in the southern part of the state. Maine covers 33,123 square miles (85,788 square kilometers). This makes it the thirty-ninth largest state.

fun fact

Maine is a good place to escape a crowd. For its size, it is the least populated state east of the Mississippi River.

New
Brunswick

Quebec

Maine

Kennebec River

Bangor

Mount Desert
Island

Augusta

Lewiston

Vermont

Portland

Atlantic
Ocean

New
Hampshire

N

W   E

S

Massachusetts

In the early 1600s, the French and English explored the area now known as Maine. Some traded furs with the Abenaki and other **Native** Americans. For about 170 years, Maine was claimed by Massachusetts. Mainers were angry when they received little help from Massachusetts during the **War of 1812**. They created their own state in 1820.

War of 1812

Maine Timeline!

1652: Massachusetts claims Maine territory. It will gain full control in 1677.

1775: British troops burn Falmouth (now Portland) as punishment for opposing the king.

1775: The first naval battle of the Revolutionary War is fought near Machias. Mainers capture the British ship *Margaretta*.

1820: Maine becomes the twenty-third state.

1832: The capital moves from Portland to Augusta.

1842: The Webster-Ashburton Treaty ends the argument over the border between Canada and Maine.

1948: Mainer Margaret Chase Smith is the first woman to be elected to both houses of the U.S. Congress.

2009: Maine's lowest temperature ever is recorded at -50 degrees Fahrenheit (-46 degrees Celsius).

burning of Falmouth

Margaret Chase Smith

Augusta

The Land

West Quoddy Head

fun fact

West Quoddy Head is the easternmost part of the United States mainland. The site is home to one of Maine's most famous lighthouses. Built in 1857, it still runs today.

Running along the northwest side of Maine are the Appalachian Mountains. These low peaks are blanketed in **evergreen** forests. Thousands of years ago, **glaciers** carved out the clear mountain lakes and narrow valleys of this region. Across the state lies the Aroostook **Plateau**. This area holds rich soil.

Maine's Climate

average °F

spring
Low: 30°
High: 51°

summer
Low: 55°
High: 75°

fall
Low: 36°
High: 55°

winter
Low: 8°
High: 28°

Coastal lowlands run along the Atlantic Ocean.
Here, sandy beaches are broken up by jagged rocks.
Hundreds of islands lie scattered off the shore. Maine
has long and snowy winters. Summers are warm and
humid, but rarely hot.

Mount Desert Island

As sailors approach Maine's coast, they see a rocky island rising out of the fog. Mount Desert Island is the state's largest island. French explorer Samuel de Champlain named it after its bare mountain tops.

The island is divided almost in two by Somes **Sound**. Glaciers carved out this deep waterway. Mount Desert Island is home to the first national park east of the Mississippi River. Each year, thousands of people visit Acadia National Park to hike, fish, and swim. The island also boasts Cadillac Mountain, the tallest peak on the North Atlantic coast.

fun fact

Early morning risers love Cadillac Mountain. It is one of the first places in the country to see the sunrise each day.

view from
Cadillac Mountain

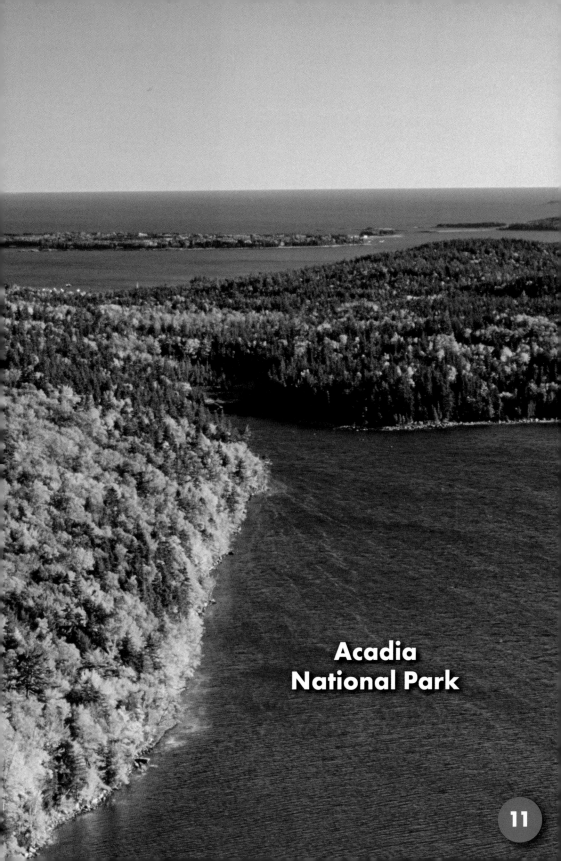

Acadia
National Park

Atlantic puffins

fun fact!

Atlantic puffins are nicknamed "clowns of the sea." Puffin nesting grounds are popular stops for sightseers in Maine.

Maine is called the Pine Tree State for good reason. Almost nine-tenths of its land is covered in trees, including white pine, spruce, and birch. Many kinds of animals make their homes in the woods. Porcupines climb trees to find food while black bears search for berries.

porcupine

Canada lynx

shrimp

In the mountains, the rare Canada lynx chases prey in deep snow. Moose stop to drink from clear lakes. Off Maine's rocky shores, clams, shrimp, and lobsters dwell in shallow bays. Farther out, whales can be seen coming up for air.

Landmarks

Mainers think big! Between Presque Isle and Houlton is the world's largest model of the solar system. From the Sun to Pluto, it covers 40 miles (64 kilometers). The world's largest spinning globe sits in Yarmouth. Named Eartha, it measures 41.5 feet (12.5 meters) from pole to pole.

In 1607, **colonists** in Maine built the first ship in North America. Visitors can learn about the state's sailing past at the Maine Maritime Museum. Maine's rich logging history comes alive at Leonard's Mills Historic Settlement. Actors show what life was like in early **lumber camps**.

solar system

Eartha

Maine Maritime Museum

Portland

With a population of more than 66,000, Portland is Maine's largest city. English settlers founded it in 1633. Throughout its history, Portland burned to the ground four times. The city went on to become an important **port**. During World Wars I and II, many **naval ships** were built there.

Old Port

Today, visitors can explore the area known as Old Port. This historic part of town has cobblestone streets and buildings that date back to the 1800s. Portland is also home to the world's first **cryptozoology** museum. Guests here can learn about mysterious creatures like Bigfoot and the Loch Ness Monster.

Working

Did you know?
The largest lobster ever caught in Maine was 3.3 feet (1 meter) long. It weighed 27 pounds (12 kilograms)!

Mainers have always relied on their state's rich **natural resources**. The vast forests are harvested to make paper and other wood products. Most farming takes place in the north. There, the soil is good for growing potatoes. Blueberries are another major crop.

Fishing and shipbuilding provide important jobs in the coastal region. Maine produces more lobsters than any other state. The lobsters and other shellfish are sold in restaurants throughout New England. Most Mainers have **service jobs**. They work in hospitals, shops, and restaurants. Many serve the millions of **tourists** that visit the state each year.

Where People Work in Maine

farming and natural resources
7%

manufacturing
3%

government
14%

services
76%

Playing

Mainers find plenty of outdoor adventures in their state. Hikers flock to the many trails and parks. In summer, beach lovers head to the coast. Sailboats explore the **coves** and islands off shore. Maine's many historic lighthouses are popular stops for visitors.

The fun doesn't stop in winter. **Snowmobiling**, ice-skating, and ice fishing are all popular winter activities. Sugarloaf Mountain Resort is the largest ski area east of the Rocky Mountains. Each year, thousands of people come to ski its trails and explore Maine's beautiful mountains.

Sugarloaf Mountain Resort

fun fact

The Appalachian Trail starts in northern Maine and stretches all the way to Georgia. This hiking path is more than 2,000 miles (3,219 kilometers) long and passes through 14 states.

Appalachian Trail

Blueberry Slump

Ingredients:

2 cups fresh Maine wild blueberries

1/2 cup sugar

1 cup water

1 cup sifted flour

2 teaspoons baking powder

1/4 teaspoon salt

1/2 cup milk

Directions:

1. Combine blueberries, sugar, and water in a saucepan. Stew over medium heat.

2. Mix flour, baking powder, and salt in a bowl. Add milk to the dry mixture, stirring quickly until dough is slightly moist.

3. When sauce is boiling, drop dough by spoonful (1 to 2 inches in size) into it. Lower heat a little and cover pan tightly. Cook for about 20 minutes.

4. Spoon dumplings into shallow bowls and cover them with sauce. Top with cream or whipped cream if desired.

lobster dinner

clam chowder

Since ancient times, fish and shellfish have been an important part of Maine cooking. Lobsters are served whole. Diners crack them open with special tools and dip the meat in melted butter. Clam **chowder** and scallop stew are also favorites, especially in winter. Mainers often buy their seafood live from local markets.

Native Americans introduced settlers to corn and beans. Today, Mainers serve these foods in dishes like hull corn soup. The state's plentiful potatoes are a common sight on dinner plates. Maine cooks dish them up boiled, baked, or fried. For something sweet, Mainers whip up blueberry slump. The state's berries are heated along with soft biscuits in this popular dessert.

Festivals

Mainers love sharing their foods, music, and **traditions** at local festivals. The Maine Boats, Homes and Harbor Show in Rockland celebrates the state's boating culture. The festival includes live music, seafood, and a dog show. The American Folk Festival in Bangor features music and dance from different cultures across the country. **Vendors** sell unique foods and handmade crafts.

American Folk Festival

Lobster Festival

The Maine Lobster Festival has been an annual tradition for more than 50 years. The five-day festival includes parades and lots of seafood. In the festival cook-off, people compete to see who can make the most delicious lobster dish.

Scrimshaw

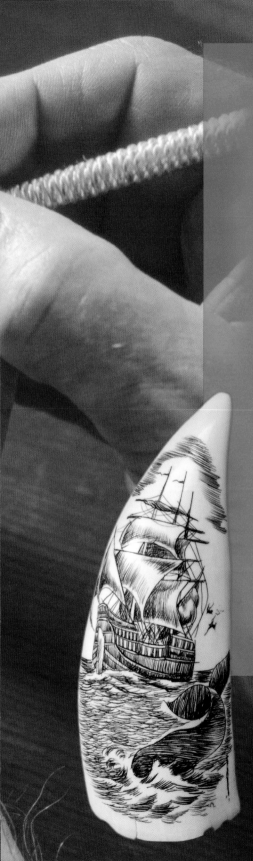

During the 1800s, many Mainers went to sea as whalers. Whaling ships could be gone for months or years. To pass the time, sailors carved pictures of life at sea into whale teeth and bones. These carvings became known as **scrimshaw**.

Commercial whaling in America ended in the 1930s, but the art of scrimshaw has been kept alive. Scrimshanders now carve mostly on the bones of other animals or on plastic. Dedicated artists buy and sell scrimshaw at art fairs and in shops. Today's scrimshaw artists carry on a proud Maine tradition.

Fast Facts About Maine

Maine's Flag

Maine's flag features the state seal in a field of blue. The seal shows a moose beneath a tall pine tree. To the right of this image is a sailor resting on an anchor. To the left is a farmer resting on a farm tool. A banner above the image displays the state motto. It wraps around the base of the North Star.

State Flower
white pine cone and tassel

State Nicknames:	The Pine Tree State The Lumber State
State Motto:	*Dirigo*; "I Direct"
Year of Statehood:	1820
Capital City:	Augusta
Other Major Cities:	Portland, Lewiston, Bangor
Population:	1,328,361 (2010)
Area:	33,123 square miles (85,788 square kilometers); Maine is the 39th largest state.
Major Industries:	services, lumber, manufacturing, fishing, farming
Natural Resources:	forests, seafood
State Government:	151 representatives; 35 senators
Federal Government:	2 representatives; 2 senators
Electoral Votes:	4

State Animal
moose

State Bird
black-capped
chickadee

Glossary

chowder—a thick, creamy soup made with seafood or vegetables

colonists—people who leave their home country to settle new land for it

commercial—done for profit

coves—sheltered areas where the shoreline dips inland

cryptozoology—the study of animals that have not been proven to exist

evergreen—a tree that stays green and does not lose its leaves in winter

glaciers—massive sheets of ice that cover large areas of land

lumber camps—small communities of lumberjacks employed to chop down trees

native—originally from a specific place

natural resources—materials in the earth that are taken out and used to make products or fuel

naval ships—ships used by a nation's navy

New England—a group of six states that make up the northeastern corner of the United States

plateau—an area of flat, raised land

port—a harbor where ships can dock

province—an area within a country; a province follows all the laws of the country and makes some of its own laws.

scrimshaw—art made by carving bones, teeth, or other material

service jobs—jobs that perform tasks for people or businesses

snowmobiling—the sport of driving snowmobiles; snowmobiles are vehicles that move quickly over snow.

sound—a long, wide extension of the ocean into land

tourists—people who travel to visit another place

traditions—customs, ideas, or beliefs handed down from one generation to the next

vendors—people who sell goods

War of 1812—a war between Britain and the United States; much of the war was fought at sea.

To Learn More

AT THE LIBRARY

Fendler, Donn. *Lost on a Mountain in Maine*. New York, N.Y.: Beech Tree Books, 1992.

Peterson, Judy Monroe. *Maine: Past and Present*. New York, N.Y.: Rosen Central, 2011.

Plourde, Lynn. *Margaret Chase Smith: A Woman for President*. Watertown, Mass.: Charlesbridge, 2008.

ON THE WEB

Learning more about Maine is as easy as 1, 2, 3.

1. Go to www.factsurfer.com.

2. Enter "Maine" into the search box.

3. Click the "Surf" button and you will see a list of related Web sites.

With factsurfer.com, finding more information is just a click away.

Index

The images in this book are reproduced through the courtesy of: Richard Cavalleri, front cover (bottom); Archive Images/ Alamy, p. 6; North Wind Picture Archives/ Alamy, p. 7 (left); (Collection)/ Prints & Photographs Division/ Library of Congress, p. 7 (middle); Zack Frank, pp. 7 (right), 10; PHB.cz (Richard Semik), p. 8; Eric Cote, pp. 8-9; Stock Connection/ SuperStock, pp. 10-11; Piotr Gatlik, pp. 12-13; Tony Rix, p. 13 (top); Dennis Donohue, p. 13 (middle); Andry Bayda, p. 13 (bottom); AP Photo/ Robert F. Bukaty/ Associated Press, p. 14 (left & right); View Pictures Ltd/ SuperStock, pp. 14-15; Visions of America/ SuperStock, pp. 16-17; Age Fotostock/ SuperStock, p. 17, 26-27; Richard Ellis/ Age Fotostock/ SuperStock, p. 18; San Rostro/ Age Fotostock, p. 19; Pat & Chuck Blackley/ Alamy, p. 20 (bottom); Exactostock/ SuperStock, p. 20 (top); Universal Images Group/ SuperStock, pp. 20-21; NightAndDayImages, p. 22; Marco Mayer, p. 23 (top); Olga Lyubkina, p. 23 (bottom); AP Photo/ Michael C. York/ Associated Press, pp. 24-25; Allison V. Smith/ Getty Images, p. 25; Glaflamme, p. 27; Pakmor, p. 28 (top); Bhathaway, p. 28 (bottom); Steve Byland, p. 29 (left); Volodymyr Burdiak, p. 29 (right).